Drummer's Guide to Big Band

by Garey Williams

Executive producers: Joe Bergamini & Dom Famularo

Edited by Joe Bergamini

Cover design: Terry Branam

Layout, book design, music engraving, and illustrations by Terry Branam

www.wizdom-media.com

WIZDOM MEDIA LLC
48 Troy Hills Rd., Whippany, NJ 07981
Copyright ©2015 Wizdom Media LLC
Exclusively distributed by Alfred Music

Contents

Drum Examples:

Performed by Garey Williams at Blissman Studios, Federal Way, WA.

Piano and horn arrangements performed by Eugene Bien.
Acoustic bass and guitar performed by Wayne Bliss.
Recorded and engineered by Wayne Bliss.
Mastered by Mike Bruce, Auricle Audio Mastering, North Bend, WA
Videographer and editing by Brian Bendetti

www.gareywilliams.com
www.drumsetartistry.com

Play-Along Charts:

Performed by the **Full Circle Jazz Ensemble**:
Nathaniel Paul Schleimer- Alto saxophone
Richard Cole and Mike West - Tenor saxophones
Jack Klitzman - Baritone saxophone
Bobby Medina and Ron Barrow - Trumpets
Bill Anthony - Trombone
Bob Hammer and Eric Verlinde - Piano
Frank Seeberger - Guitar
Wayne Bliss - Acoustic bass
Garey Williams - Drums
Bernie Jacobs and Stephanie Porter - Vocals

All Rights Reserved.

Recorded at David Lang Studios, Puyallup, WA
Recording engineer - David Lang
Mixed by Wayne Bliss, Blissman Studios, Federal Way, WA
Mastered by Mike Bruce, Auricle Audio Mastering, North Bend, WA

Bella's Boogie performed by **The Jim Cutler Jazz Orchestra**:
Jim Cutler (Lead), Gordon Brown - Alto saxophones
Mike West, Paul Gillespie - Tenor saxophones
James DeJoie - Baritone saxophone
Chris Amemiya (Lead), Steve Kirk, Kress Fransen - Trombones
Bill Park - Bass trombone
Mike Mines (Lead), Peter Kirkman, Al Keith, Daniel Barry - Trumpets
Gregg Robinson - Piano
Philip Demaree - Bass
Garey Williams - Drums

All Rights Reserved.

Recorded at Studio X, Seattle, WA
Recording engineers - Reed Ruddy, Sam Hofstedt
Edited and Mixed by - Dave Pascal

Dedication

This book is dedicated to the memory of "Coach" John Moawad. John Moawad was a professional jazz drummer, jazz vocalist, classical percussionist and timpanist prior to becoming the Jazz Studies Director and Percussion Instructor at Central Washington University from 1970-1998.

John Moawad was a "walking encyclopedia" of jazz. He amassed an enormous collection of recordings, big band and vocal jazz ensemble charts and videos. His knowledge of jazz was so extensive that he could tell you names of band members, singers, what bands they were in, the years they played, what recordings they were on and more!

From 1981-1985, I was fortunate to be the drummer for John Moawad's, Central Washington University Jazz Band 1. During rehearsals he would often play the drums for for me to show me exactly how to interpret big band drum charts and lead a big band. He would say, "You have to learn how to drive the bus!" I literally had big band drumming lessons right there with the big band. It was the best education possible.

He taught me how to "kick the band" with many different kinds of set-ups. He introduced me to numerous recordings and would often stress the importance of playing authentically. "You have to learn to wear the hats," he would often say— referring to listening to the great drummers and learning how to play in a variety of styles of music. He taught me the importance of dynamics and getting a good drum sound that complimented the sound of the band and style of music. John Moawad told me, "Pick a drummer you like. Get as many recordings as you can with that drummer. Listen and get to the point where you feel you have learned everything you can from that drummer. Then pick another drummer and do it all over again."

Dedication

He had little patience for rhythmic errors saying, "Do the math on your own time. When you are in here (the rehearsal) we work on music and interpretation, not rhythms." He taught me how to listen and accompany a soloist; how to play the ride cymbal, china cymbal and hi hats; how to play behind saxophone solis; and how to "put it to bed" with the bass drum at the end of a ballad. One of his statements about chart reading and performing was, "You have to stay focused from count-off to cut-off." These are just a few examples of his many teachings.

John Moawad would often say, "Spread the wealth. Share your knowledge. Help your brothers and sisters." I owe A LOT to this man and I am thrilled to be able to pass along his teachings to you.

"Garey is one of the finest drummers I've ever worked with, but he is probably the best drum set teacher I've helped produce."

- John Moawad

Acknowledgments

I would like to thank the key teachers and musicians that inspired my interest and education in big band drumming and music: my father, Burton J. Williams, for taking me to big band concerts while I was in grade school; the late Professor John Moawad for encouragement, understanding and providing a priceless education by playing drums for me in jazz band so many times to show me how it is done; Jeff Hamilton for encouraging me to pursue a jazz drumming career, teaching me some amazing brushes, how to relax, and how to get a great cymbal sound; Bruce Babad for your encouragement and support and all those great gigs!; Bob Hammer for the great compositions and arrangements; Nathaniel Paul Schleimer for making the Full Circle Jazz Ensemble come to life; Wayne Bliss for your excellent bass playing and recording skills; Eugene Bien for the tasty piano and horn arrangements; Brian Benedetti for his excellent videographer skills; and my wife, Valerie, for her unending support.

Foreword

Since meeting Garey at a jazz camp in the early '80s as a young jazz participant in Port Townsend, Washington, I have admired his commitment and dedication to nurturing his talents.

His attention to detail, while striving for perfection, is shared with you in this book. By paying close attention to his great organizational skills, you'll benefit greatly by following his advice.

The information that follows is the result of Garey being an eternal student of the music. As the great drummer—and another "eternal student"—Shelly Manne shared with me, "If you stop asking questions about this music, it's time to hang up the sticks and brushes." Garey has always been hungry to learn the history of this "beast" of an instrument, as well as being a part of where it may lead us.

Enjoy your journey through this informative book!

Jeff Hamilton

About the Author

Garey Williams has played drums professionally in the Northwest since the 1980s working with numerous bands and many notable jazz musicians including Diana Krall, Kristin Korb, Bud Shank, Barney McClure, Howard Roberts, Joe Williams, Dizzy Gillespie, Clay Jenkins, Inger Jensen, Eddie Daniels, Jay Thomas, Bob Nixon, Bob Hammer, Milo Petersen, Bernie Jacobs, Eric Verlinde, John Hansen, Kelley Johnson, Greta Metassa, Karin Shivers, Trish Hadley, Gale Pettis, Jacqueline Tabor, Alexey Nikolaev, Chris Spencer, Jake Bergevin, Bill Anschell, Johnny Conga, Michael Powers, Darren Motamody, Geoffrey Castle, The Jim Cutler jazz Orchestra, The Jazz Police, The Full Circle Jazz Ensemble, the Seattle Repertory Jazz Orchestra, as well as many other stars of the local scene.

As a drummer and educator, Garey has become one of the most sought after teachers and performers in the Northwest. Garey received his Masters of Music in Percussion Performance & Jazz Studies from Central Washington University in 1993 and Garey was a member of the CWU music faculty between 1999-2001, teaching orchestral percussion and drumset, percussion methods, percussion ensemble, jazz band and jazz history.

In 2009, Garey returned to Seattle to continue his career as a performer and educator. He has performed in countless festival and concert venues, including the Bite of Seattle, the Jazz in the Valley Festival, the Port Townsend Jazz Festival, the Banff Jazz Festival, and many other Northwest festivals. In 2001 - 2012 Garey was a member of the jazz fusion trio Ecstasy In Numbers and has been reviewed in *Modern Drummer*, *Rhythm Magazine*, *Percussive Notes*, and numerous regional and local newspapers. As a studio musician, Garey has recorded over 50 commercial CDs and has done sessions for radio and television.

Garey is an active public school clinician presenting clinics in over one hundred schools. He has taught numerous master classes and clinics at universities, music stores, drum shops, drum schools, jazz camps and jazz festivals. Garey endorses and conducts clinics for DW drums, Crescent cymbals, Regal Tip sticks, Remo drumheads and Latin Percussion, and is the author of *The Hi-Hat Foot* (published by Wizdom Media and distributed by Alfred). Currently, Garey teaches drumset at the Edmonds Community College, Central Washington University, Lakeside School and at his home studio in Seattle, WA.

About the Book

Drummers Guide to Big Band was written to help drummers and educators understand how to interpret and play big band charts.

You will be taught a three-step process to chart interpretation called the Chart Reading Checklist: Style, Road Map, and Ink. There are video demonstrations on how to play big band set-ups that will clearly and effectively support the band. The jazz swing and shuffle feels are demonstrated, as are brush techniques for ballad and swing tempi. Viewers will also be shown three jazz ride cymbal techniques for three tempo ranges: slow, medium-fast and fast.

You will be given tips on how to select jazz cymbals, jazz drumsticks, brushes and mallets. Hi-hat stick and pedal techniques will be demonstrated on the accompanying video/MP3 disc, and you will learn how to coordinate the open/closed, hand and hand/foot techniques used to play a two-beat hi-hat pattern. Rocking-the-foot and heel-up pedal techniques will be explained and demonstrated.

You will learn how to "feather" the bass drum with a heel-down approach and how to "drop bombs" with a heel-up approach, and will learn to apply a combination of these two pedal techniques. The two-beat and "four-on-the-floor" bass drum methods are explained and demonstrated.

Snare drum "colors" such as rim shots are demonstrated; these are great for set-ups. The cross-stick technique is demonstrated; this is great for laying down a swinging 2-and-4 groove and necessary for many Latin rhythms. Stick shots are also an important color the big band drummer needs to be able to execute; these are great for pickup rhythms at the beginning of phrases and solos.

This book focuses on jazz in 4/4 and 3/4 time signatures. Several different jazz swing feels and jazz shuffle feels are discussed and demonstrated in 4/4 time. You will learn how to interpret 3/4 time signatures: when to play with a "one" feel, a "three" feel or a "two" feel (polyrhythm).

Brushes for ballads, two-beat, and swing feels are explained and demonstrated.

There are also some additional drumming styles that today's big band drummer needs to be able to play. For each drumming style there are musical play-along tracks and charts that I will demonstrate and that you can play along with.
There are five big band selections, each with a chart, MP3 with the full band, and an MP3 without the drums. These charts will give you a realistic big band playing experience. Study the charts and the recordings and try to incorporate the various concepts found in this book.

About the Disc

The included MP3/MP4 audio/video disc contains demonstrations of all of the exercises in this book. The audio tracks are set up so you can practice along with them. The MP3s can be played with any audio software, and the videos can be played with any video software that plays MP4s. For best results, we recommend iTunes and QuickTime to open these files. These MP3s will play like a normal CD in newer CD players. If they won't play in your CD player, simply put the disc in your computer and import the tracks into iTunes or your favorite music software. The videos are in a folder entitled "DG to Big Band Videos." To play a video, navigate to that folder on the disc, open it, and double click an MP4 video file to open it.

On pages 24-29, each track begins with two bars of click. Exercises 1-8 (in 4/4 time) and exercises 9-14 (in 3/4 time) are played using a 12-bar blues form. You will hear play each four-bar exercise a total of six times (6 x 4 = 24). This amounts to two 12-bar blues forms. (See the chord chart on page 37.) One time through the 12-bar blues form is also referred to as "one chorus." Therefore, I play two choruses of the blues. This is followed by two more choruses of the blues without me playing—so when working with this recording, I play the first two choruses and you play the next two choruses without me. Play along with me and then play alone. Record yourself and listen back; compare your performance to mine. If we are together, then you are right on.

Each exercise in Part Five: Setting up the Big Band is played at three different tempos: slow, medium and fast. The exercises can be played using sticks or brushes. You can play with a jazz feel or a jazz shuffle feel. I will demonstrate these as I go through the exercises. There will be an icon next to each exercise identifying the track number on the disc.

For Part Six: Embellishments, I will demonstrate each embellishment using exercise 1 (from the 4/4 section). You can apply the embellishments to all of the 4/4 and 3/4 exercises. You can play along with me and then without me.

There are two charts that use a combination of big band figures, one in 4/4 and the other in 3/4. You can use either a snare drum or bass drum set-up, or any of the embellishments set-ups I explain in the text. I will demonstrate a combination of set-ups, and then you can try copying me and/or using your own set-ups.

In, Part Seven: Jazz Drumming Styles and Part Eight: Additional Drumming Styles, there are charts and play-along tracks for each style.

How to Practice

Enthusiasm is your fuel to improve! In your enthusiasm to improve your drumming, you probably spend time working on grooves and fills, playing along with recordings, searching YouTube for drumming videos, attending shows and concerts, practicing from methods books, and jamming with other musicians. Though these are all key ingredients to becoming a good drummer, the way in which you divide your time among these things, and the structure of your practice routine, determines the quality and speed of your development. Following are some suggestions that may assist you in getting the most out of your practice time. I recommend that you read through the information twice. First, to understand how to plan a practice routine. Second, to fill out the practice chart. You may want to photocopy the practice chart so you can update it as you improve.

Listen, practice and play. When developing your skills on the drumset, there are three main areas to consider. They are: listening, practicing and playing.

Listen, listen and listen some more! It may not be convenient or desirable to practice every day. On days when you aren't practicing, spend your time doing extra listening. If you're rehearsing or performing, you may not have time to practice that day. This is normal and all right. Remember, the three main categories of development are listening, practicing and playing; all are of equal importance. The goal of practicing is to become a better drummer. Practice technique, reading and coordination exercises but allow time at the end of your practice session to develop ideas and creativity. Playing time is where these ideas and skills can be refined and polished. Of course, listening is where you will gain many ideas to add to your musical drumming vocabulary, especially if you can watch and listen simultaneously. You will remember more of what you hear if you can see it happening. Ideally, spend equal amounts of time listening, practicing and playing.

First begin by making a list of what you want to learn. To best determine what to listen to, practice and play, start by making a list of all the things you want to learn. Such things might be: learning rudiments, better four limb coordination, bass drum technique, fills, grooves, etc. List all of the things you can think of on the practice chart.

Second, make a list of the things you want to improve. I feel it's helpful to distinguish between the things you can play that could be improved versus the things you have yet to learn. It may require some thought to determine what things fit into these categories. That's OK. Be thorough—it can save time in the long run.

How to Practice

Third, name six bands or artists you would ideally like to play with. You might like several kinds of music. The point of naming six groups is to focus in on what styles or genres of music you prefer. Determining the groups and/or musicians you want to play with will also help in prioritizing what things to practice.

Finally, establish short- and long-term goals. Short-term goals may be "by next month I want to...." or even shorter periods of time such as "by next week I will be able to play...." etc. Long-term goals may be "by next year I want to audition to get into a rock band," or lifelong goals such as a goal to become a studio drummer, etc. Setting goals can give you a sense of purpose and direction to your playing. This is a rewarding experience, as it builds confidence when these goals are achieved.

Plan the work, and then work the plan! Once you have determined what to learn and improve and whom you strive to play with and when, you are now ready to organize this information into a workable practice routine.

How much time do you want to practice each day? To begin with, decide how much time you want to practice. You must be sure this amount of time is realistic and comfortable for you. There may be a difference in how much time you want to practice versus the amount of time you have available to practice. The amount of time is less important than the quality. Practice for results.

What time of day are you going to practice? Next, decide what time of day you can commit to practice on a regular basis. Reserving a certain practice time each day will ensure it gets accomplished.

Practice what you want to perform now. Select those things from your list that relate to your present playing opportunities. If you're not playing with a group, practice the things that will help you to play with the groups you have listed.

Balance your practice diet. In the process of selecting what to practice, I strongly suggest choosing things that develop your technique, reading and coordination. Becoming a great drummer requires that you develop a high level of technical facility (rudimental capabilities), reading skills (counting and sight reading), and coordination skills, the beginning of which this book will discuss and develop.

How to Practice

Become a drumming artist. It's very important to schedule time to be creative! This time can be spent on making up drumbeats, soloing, combining different styles of grooves, etc. In the "real world" of performing, your success depends on your interpretation of the music and your style of playing. If your practice time is spent only working through method books, where you are following written beats or patterns, your creative, interpretive and unique style of playing may be underdeveloped. Simply block off a portion of your practice time to experiment as well as test your recall of the beats you've been working on out of the text you're studying. When you're making up beats or soloing, etc., try to imagine that you're playing with a group (playing phrases, the form, fills, etc.). This will help you to transfer your ideas musically to a playing situation with other musicians. "hear" the sound of the groove/music in your mind. You will play what you hear internally.

Create the practice routine. Now it's time to decide the order of things to practice. I recommend starting with your least favorite subject and ending with your most favorite activities. Subjects that you feel are necessary to practice are not always the most fun. Simply put, save dessert for last.

Following is an example of how you might organize a one hour daily practice routine:

10-15 minutes of technique followed by...
10-15 minutes of reading material followed by...
10-15 minutes of coordination develoment followed by...
10-20 minutes of experimentation.

Practice makes permanent. More important than the total amount of time you practice is the consistency of that practice time. The more consistent you are in your studies, the easier, more obvious and rapid will be your development. Once you've arrived at a practice schedule, stick to it. You will find that modifying or even changing your schedule will come as you progress. In the beginning, however, commitment is the key to successful development. I recommend calculating your progress on a weekly, not daily basis. You may struggle with something one day, and then play it with ease the next. If so, you are not alone. Some days are better than others. The experienced musician realizes this and makes the best of it.

Post the practice routine in writing where you can see it. Finally, when your practice schedule is finalized and written down, place it where you can see it. This will help you avoid wasting any time trying to remember what to practice, when and for how long.

I believe if you make the effort to be efficient, determined and enthusiastic you will surely see progress. Organization is the key to success!

Practice Chart

Things that I want to learn:	
1	6
2	7
3	8
4	9
5	10

Things that I would like to improve:	
1	6
2	7
3	8
4	9
5	10

Six groups or artists that I would like to play with :	
1	4
2	5
3	6

Short-term goals	Long-term goals

Practice Schedule

Practice Amount:		Time of day:	
Time	Description	Time	Description
1		6	
2		7	
3		8	
4		9	
5		10	

Part One: The Role of the Big Band Drummer

What is a big band? Big band is a term applied to a large group of woodwind, brass, and rhythm section instruments playing together. A big band is sometimes referred to as a stage band, lab band, jazz band or reading band. Big bands are typically composed of four sections of instruments with five players in each section: saxophones (woodwinds), two brass sections, trombones (low brass) & trumpets (high brass) and the rhythm section.

The rhythm section is typically composed of a drummer, bassist, pianist, guitar and sometimes additional percussion instruments such as congas, shakers, vibes, etc.

Each member of the big band will be reading music, also referred to as charts, for each piece of music the band plays. BIg bands are common in middle schools, junior high schools, high schools, colleges and numerous university music programs have at least one big band ensemble if not several.

The sound of the big band is unlike any other ensemble. The size will affect the sound and the way the drummer will steer the ensemble. The big band can cover a wide variety of musical styles: jazz, funk, rock, R&B and world beat rhythms.

How do you learn to play drums in a big band? Listen!
The sound of music answers more question than a chart can provide alone. You learned how to talk before you learned how to read. Listening is how you learn any auditory language. Hearing first, speaking second and reading third. There are numerous big band recordings that have been documented in audio and video forms. A simple Internet search will reveal what's available, along with the discography on page 51.

However, I recommend you begin by listening to the recordings of the chart(s) you will be expected to rehearse and perform. Ask your big band director to provide you with a recording or information on how you can obtain a recording. Some charts will have the publishers information at the bottom. Find the publisher's website. They will often provide an MP3 audio sample or complete recording of the chart.

How do you learn to read big band drum charts? Listen while looking!
Have the drum chart in front of you and, while listening to the recording, follow along with the chart. This is the clearest way to understand and learn how the drummer interpreted the music, I.e. what rhythms are played on what parts of the drumset and how. Have a pencil in hand and write notes, words or symbols to help you remember which notes to play short and which notes to play long. I would often circle the notes that I wanted to crash based upon what I heard the drummer on the recording doing.

Part One

There are so many styles of music that it is essential to hear a recording. To understand how to interpret the chart you need to both listen and look at the chart. There is a "vocabulary" to every style of music. The sound of the cymbals, the drums and the way they are played. You need to learn the authentic vocabulary before trying to "speak" it on the drums. Authentic means the correct sound, feel and touch, while supporting the various horn sections, ensemble sections, soloists and other members of the rhythm section within the style of the music being played.

Connect sound with sight! Repeated listening to the chart(s) you will be playing will help you memorize the sound of the music. Once you have the sound of the music in your head, you can follow the chart and better understand how the drummer arrived at his or her recorded performance. The end result of this process of listening to the recording while following along in the chart will develop your ability to hear with your eyes.

Are there different kinds of drum charts? Yes! (That is why the recording is so important.) There is no standardized method that arrangers use to write drum charts. Some charts can be basic or complex, depending upon the composer and/or arranger. You may be given some information about the feel, tempo and sometimes suggested or even written beats. The drum chart is written as a guide to the rhythm, melody and harmony of the music. The rhythm parts that are written out are often what the other instruments are playing. The drummer's job is to react to the rhythms in a way that best supports the band musically.

By listening to the recording and following the chart you will learn how the rehearsal letters or numbers relate to the musical sections of the composition: the introduction, melody, solo sections and background instruments, shout choruses, dynamics, feel/ style changes, etc. Listen and locate these phrase points on the chart. Internalize the melody and what section of the ensemble is playing the melody. Internalize the form: either a 12-bar blues, AABA or other forms unique to the arrangement. This will help you see how the chart is simply a musical description or outline of the sound you are hearing. I recommend you write a little number (4, 8, 12, or 4, 8, 12,16, etc.) over every four measures. This can really help to keep track of where you are in the phrases. Place the music stand to the left of the hi-hat stand so that you can clearly read the charts and be able to turn pages when necessary.

Part One

The feel, steadiness in tempo and attention to dynamics will have the greatest benefit to the band as a whole. Overplaying with a busy groove and the overuse of fills, can overshadow the melody, harmony and flow of the music. The drummer leads the ensemble with dynamics. Your dynamic approach to a phrase or rhythmic figure will be mirrored by the band. If they can't hear you, they will adjust their volume to you. On the contrary, if you can't hear the ensemble, then you may be playing too loud.

Thinking musically means thinking melodically, harmonically and dynamically. Hear the melody, harmony and dynamics! Be able to hear and even sing the melody in your head at the volume level it is played at. Hear the repetitive harmonic chord progressions that outline the phrases within the song's form. Drums are not considered a melodic or harmonic instrument. However, when the drummer plays the dynamic contour of the melody it gives the listener the sound of playing the drums melodically.

For example, if the melody is ascending or in the upper register, respond by matching the volume, timbres or pitches on the drums and cymbals. Low melodic lines and chords can be played on lower sounds of the drumset.

Mark the phrase points. The drummer needs to always know where the phrases begin and end. It is the harmony or chord progression that outlines the phrase lengths. The drummer will often "mark" the phrase points with cymbal accents, a fill, a change in feel, cymbal sounds, and/or dynamics. Sometimes consulting the lead trumpet part will give you the best melodic and dynamic information to help you create the most musical drum part.

Long and short notes = Long and short sounds. The length of the notes played by the other instruments should also be considered and even mirrored by your playing. It's important to imitate how long a note or chord is played by choosing long or short sounds on the drumset. Short notes can be played on the snare drum or closed hats or a choked cymbal sound. Long notes can be played on bass drum, toms and cymbals. These short and long sounds are referred to as *articulations*. Similar to enunciation when speaking, try to be as musically articulate as possible. This way you will be communicating the melody and harmony as clearly as possible. You will learn a variety of ways to do this by listening to and playing big band music.

Getting the big band drum sound makes a big difference! The sound of the music is affected by the sound of the drums and, especially the sound of your cymbals. Since the foundation of the big band is based upon the sound of acoustic instruments such as saxophones, trombones, trumpets, acoustic piano and acoustic bass, the sound of the drums should have a clear ring and projection that also blends with the sonic qualities of all the other instruments. As a comparison, this is not the same sound the drummer would use in a rock band with electric guitars, electric bass, a singer with amplification through a loud PA system. On the contrary, the big band drummer will be playing a lot of jazz and often at a soft volume level. Brush playing is required as well. The use of mallets and sometimes even various wood bundles and other sounds effects may be asked for. I have even played with my hands.

Jazz drums and cymbals: Following is a list of equipment the big band drummer needs to effectively lead the ensemble.

Drums:

Four-piece jazz drumset: 14" snare; 12" or 13" mounted tom; 14" or 16" floor tom; and 22", 20" or 18" bass drum. All drums should have coated or similar heads that produce a clear sound when played with brushes.

Cymbals:

14" hi-hats, 18-20" ride/crash on left side, 20-22" ride on right side, 22" Chinese cymbal with rivets; an 8-12" splash and 16-18" crash are optional.

Hardware:

Straight cymbal stands with single braced legs are all that is needed. A quality screw-height-adjustable drum throne is essential. Posture is very important and affects coordination. A carpet is needed to keep the hi-hat stand and/or bass drum from sliding due to pressing on the pedals. A felt beater is recommended for the bass drum pedal.

Sticks, Brushes and Mallets:

Wood tip sticks (2 pairs), wire brushes and felt mallets.

Part Two: Chart Analysis and Interpretation

What to do when handed a big band drum chart. When handed a chart, it is important to gain as much information as possible in the shortest time possible. You will not always have time to listen to a recording. You will need to rely on the chart alone. Before playing the chart there are several things you want to look for and in a specific order. I have divided these items into three categories called the Chart Reading Checklist:

1. Style:

a. Feel/Time Signature - Rhythm is the foundation to all music! What is the proper feel and style of groove you need to create and in what time signature (4/4, ¢, ¢, 3/4 swing, two-beat, shuffle, samba, Afro-Cuban 6/8, R&B, etc.)? Some arrangers will write the feel in words at the top of the chart. Other times it may be implied in the way the notation is written. You need to know this before you can play effectively. Ask if it is not clear. The bass player's chart can help as well. The arranger may also specify brushes or mallets instead of sticks, especially for ballads.

b. Tempo - How fast or slow you play a style of music can have a dramatic effect of the choice of grooves and dynamics you can play, and the techniques and coordination involved to create the proper feel. Simplifying a groove may be necessary at faster tempos.

c. Dynamics - Are you whispering, talking, speaking loudly or shouting? The volume you play at or the *dynamic shaping* you use is one of the few devices a drummer has to giving the music more emotion. Communicate with your hands and feet the way you would with your voice.

2. Road Map Signs:

a. DS (Dal Segno) - Go back to the 𝄋 sign in the chart.
b. DC (Da Capo) - Go back to the beginning of the chart.
c. Coda ⊕ - Go to the coda near the end or at the very end of the chart.
d. Fine - End.
e. 1st & 2nd Endings or more - The number of times a phrase is played and ends.
f. Phrase Lengths/Form:
    a.) 32-Bar AABA Form - Contains four eight-bar phrases, with 16 bars of A followed by 8 bars of B, then 8 bars of A.
    b.) 12-Bar Blues Form - Contains 12 bar phrases that continually repeat.
    c.) There are also many other forms; look at your chart to determine which form it is.
g. Rit. or Ritard - Gradually slow down.
h. Fermata ⌢ - Hold out the note.

i. A Tempo - Resume previous tempo.

j. Time Signature/Feel/Style Changes - Indicated in the new time signature by the notation and/or with words: swing to Latin, half time to double time, two-feel to four-feel, etc.

k. Dynamics - Musically appropriate volume in which you play the drums and cymbals.

l. 1st or 2nd X only - Indicating to play the figures either the 1st or 2nd time through.

m. Fill - Indicating a place in the music for the drummer to play a fill.

n. Solo - Where you are featured or another member of the band is featured.

o. Tacet - Don't play; rest or quiet.

p. Vamp - Repeat a section or phrase until given a cue to go on.

q. Open - Also sometimes written as "open for solos." A section that will repeat any given number times while various members of the ensemble solo; you will go on to the next section of the chart when cued by the leader.

r. Simile - Continue in a similar manner.

s. Tutti - Together with everyone.

t. Orchestrate - How you choose to play the drums and cymbals to go with the written part.

u. Groove - Play at a steady tempo, with good feel and appropriate variations in the sound and dynamics.

3. Ink:

The term *ink* refers to the measure that contain specific rhythms/figures and terms. There are two kinds of figures in jazz band charts:

Section Figures
Ensemble Figures

Section figures **are rhythms written above the staff.** (Note: Occasionally trombone, bass or other figures may be written below the staff as well.) The drummer's role is to "catch" these rhythms by playing them on the snare drum or bass drum. Sometimes the abbreviations *trpts.* (trumpets), *sxs.* (saxophones) or *trmbs.* (trombones), are placed in parentheses next to the figures. This indicates which section of the ensemble will be playing these rhythms.

With section figures, the role of the drummer is to keep the time going on the ride cymbal and/or hi-hat, and for:

a.) Trumpet figures - "catch" with SD.

b.) Trombone figures - "catch" with BD.

c.) Saxophone figures - "catch" with either SD or BD.

d.) Play the SD for short notes , the BD for long notes.

    Short notes = Eighth notes or short/staccato quarter notes.

    Long notes = Notes with long articulations, ties, dotted quarter notes and longer note values.

Part Two

Ensemble figures **are rhythms written in or on the staff, though sometimes above the staff as well.** The drummers role is to "set-up" or "kick" these figures with fills using the snare drum, tom tom, floor tom, bass drum and crashing the cymbals, either with bass drum or snare drum. (Avoid striking all three.)

With ensemble figures the role of the drummer is to briefly stop playing time, play a fill that supports the style, dynamic and direction of the music. The fill should:

a.) End on the beat before the figure so that the band can easily hear and feel where the figure begins and where they should play.

b.) Support figures with crash/snare drum or crash/bass drum (avoid using all three voices at once).

c.) The length of the set-up can relate to the length of the figure.

Short Figures = Short Set-Ups
Long Figures = Long Set-Ups

Solo Sections. Many charts contain a solo section where the rhythm section is backing a soloist in more of a combo or small group format. The drummers role is to listen, respond to and interact with the soloist while keeping your place in the form of the music. When a smaller group of musicians are playing, the drummer has more room to add comping ideas and interact with the soloist in a "busier" manner. Choosing the right cymbals, comping behind the soloists, dynamics, etc. are all important considerations when playing behind the unique sound and range of the various solo instruments. In some cases, brushes may be more appropriate than sticks. If possible, look at the soloists if you can. We tend to listen to what we are looking at.

What if there is no drum chart? Get the lead trumpet music. Drummers need to work closely with the lead trumpet player for dynamics, articulations, etc. It's a good idea to compare a drum chart with a lead trumpet part to see how closely many of the ensemble figures relate to what is written on your drum chart. Attend sectionals by each of the sections: trumpets, trombones and saxophones to learn more about what they are playing. Your playing needs to be a reaction to what's going on around you. Hear the music as the audience would, one band-one sound, not just your part alone. The more musicians you are playing with, the less you need to play.

Part Three: Chart Symbols - The Road Map

Charts contain symbols and terms that we react to. The *road map* is an expression often used to designate where a chart begins, ends and the symbols and musical shorthand terms that the big band drummer needs to understand and learn. The more familiar you are with the "language" of charts, the more you can focus on listening. Following is a list of common terms, their definition and a notation symbol for each:

Time Slashes = Keep time while listening:

Measure Repeat = Repeat the preceding measure:

Two-Measure Repeat = Repeat the two preceding measures:

Double Bar = Phrase points in the music between sections:

Rehearsal Letters or Numbers = A ,B, C, etc. or 9, 17 or 13, 25, etc. Indicate where to begin rehearsing. Often these are at the beginning of phrases:

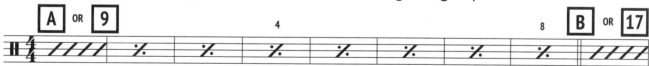

Repeat Signs = Replay the measures between the repeat signs or repeat back to a phrase point, sometimes repeating several times:

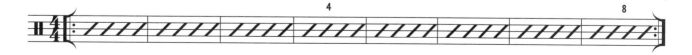

Part Three

1st & 2nd Endings = The end of the phrase will be different the first time from the second time, indicated by the bracket over the measures in each ending. Take the 1st ending the first time through, then repeat. On the second time through take the 2nd ending:

Section Figures = Sometimes referred to as *background figures*, and are written above the staff. Play the figure on the SD or BD at the appropriate background volume:

Ensemble Figures = All three horn sections or the entire ensemble of horns will play the figure and it is written in or on the staff:

Fill = Play a fill for the suggested amount of time indicated:

Solo = Play a solo in the style of and for the designated amount of measures indicated.

Part Four: Articulation Markings - The Duration of Notes

Articulation markings affect the volume and length of notes. Regardless of the style of music and the dynamic level the music is played at, there are four primary *articulation markings*:

1. Legato Marking = the note should be played long.

2. Staccato Marking = the note should be played short.

3. Accent Marking = the note should be louder; accentuate.

4. Strong Short Accent Marking = the Note should be stronger and shorter than the normal Accent.

Sometimes you see more than one articulation marking over the same note. The drummers goal is match the long and short sounds of the horn parts. Listening to the sound of the band will give you the exact articulations, even if the chart does not indicate them.

Your ears know! Record your rehearsals and performances, listen back and make adjustments to improve and/or fine tune your playing and interpretation. Take advantage of their intelligence to help you improve your sound. Compare your performance to that of the recordings you study. This is the best way to develop a more musical approach to your drumming.

Key

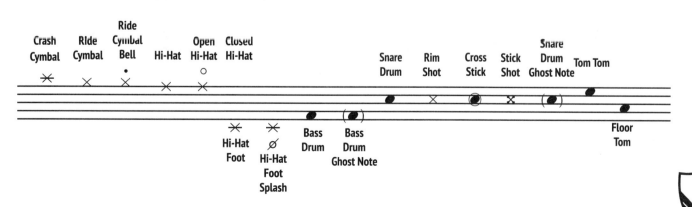

Part Five: Setting Up the Big Band

There are a variety of set-up fills a drummer can choose to play to support a **big band figure.** To begin this process lets start with a quarter note set-up played either on the snare drum or the bass drum, followed by a crash with a snare drum or bass drum on the figure the band will be playing.

There are eight beginning rhythms the drummer needs to learn to set up the big band:

> **a. Four "on" the beat rhythms: "on" beats 1, 2, 3, 4**
> **b. Four "off" the beat rhythms: On the "off" beats of 1, 2, 3, 4**

Practice through each set-up in the following way:

> **a. With a SD set-up, then crash the figure with the cymbal and BD**
> **b. With a BD set-up, then crash the figure with the cymbal and SD**

Example 1 Track 1, 2, 3

A - As written:

B - Played as SD set-up:

C - Played as BD set-up:

Example 2 Track 4, 5, 6

A - As written:

B - Played as SD set-up:

C - Played as BD set-up:

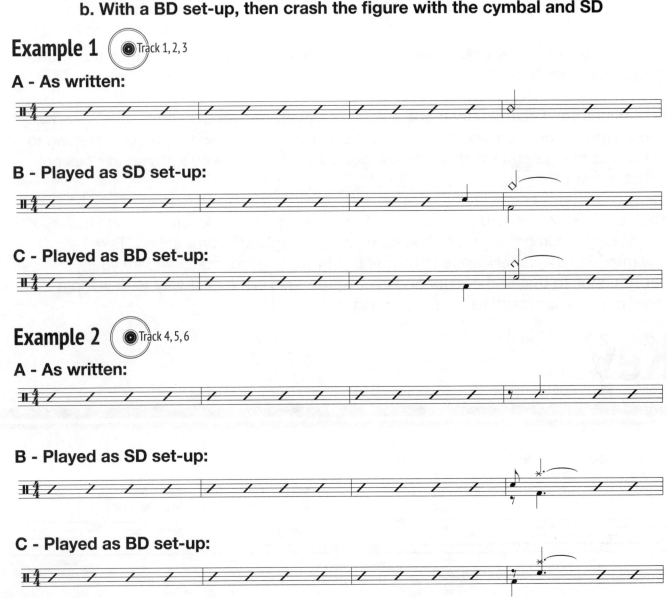

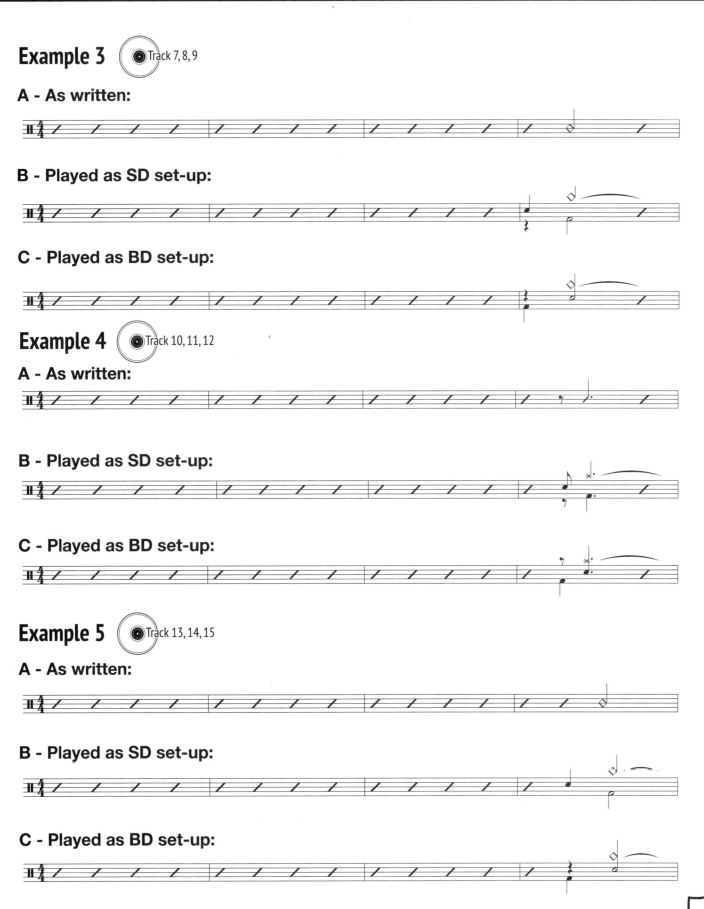

Example 3   Track 7, 8, 9

A - As written:

B - Played as SD set-up:

C - Played as BD set-up:

Example 4   Track 10, 11, 12

A - As written:

B - Played as SD set-up:

C - Played as BD set-up:

Example 5   Track 13, 14, 15

A - As written:

B - Played as SD set-up:

C - Played as BD set-up:

Part Five

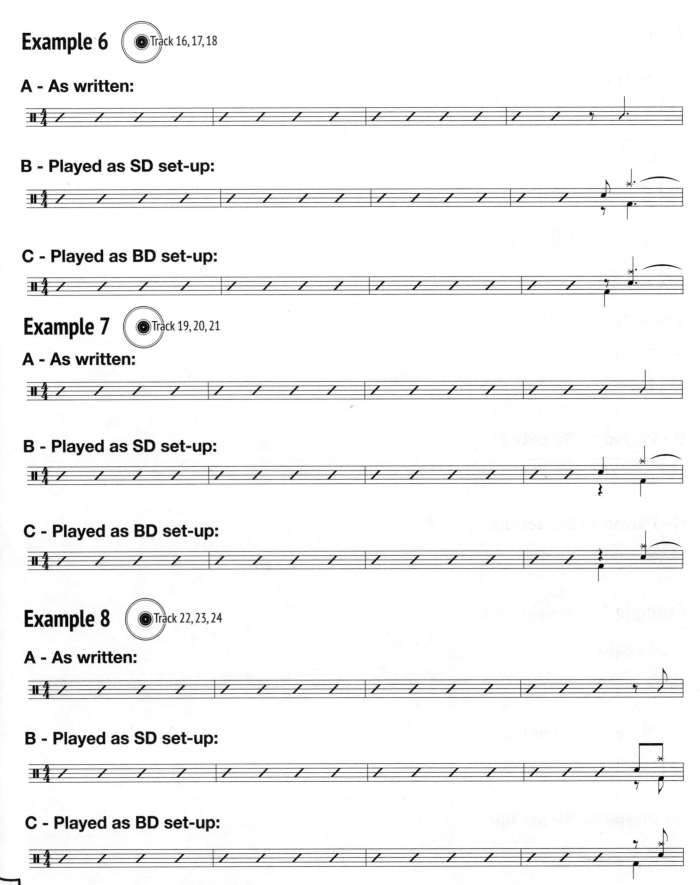

Example 6 Track 16, 17, 18

A - As written:

B - Played as SD set-up:

C - Played as BD set-up:

Example 7 Track 19, 20, 21

A - As written:

B - Played as SD set-up:

C - Played as BD set-up:

Example 8 Track 22, 23, 24

A - As written:

B - Played as SD set-up:

C - Played as BD set-up:

Example 9 Track 25, 26, 27

A - As written:

B - Played as SD set-up:

C - Played as BD set-up:

Example 10 Track 28, 29, 30

A - As written:

B - Played as SD set-up:

C - Played as BD set-up:

Example 11 Track 31, 32, 33

A - As written:

B - Played as SD set-up:

C - Played as BD set-up:

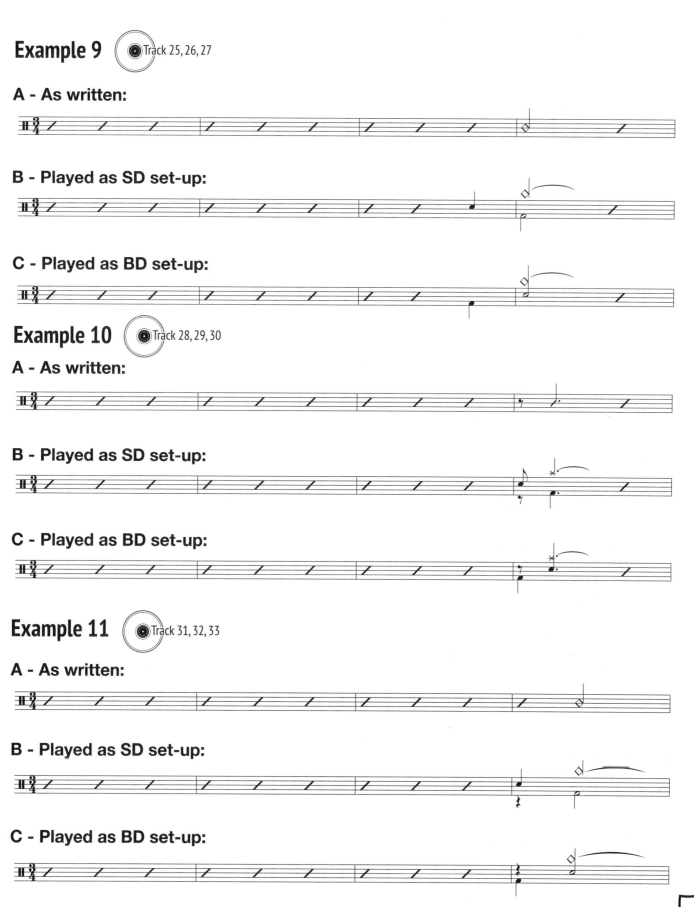

Part Five

Example 12 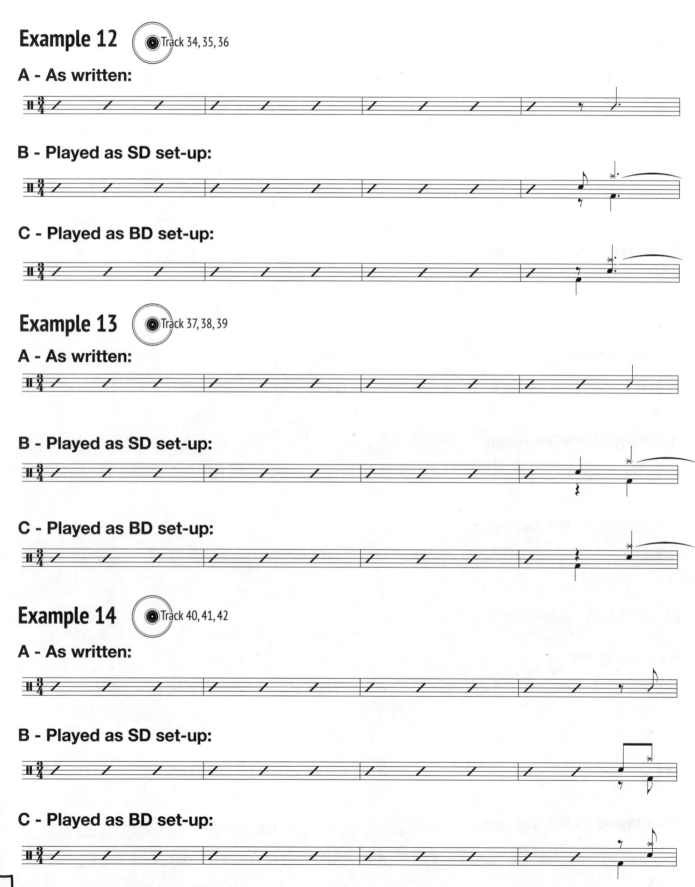 Track 34, 35, 36

A - As written:

B - Played as SD set-up:

C - Played as BD set-up:

Example 13 Track 37, 38, 39

A - As written:

B - Played as SD set-up:

C - Played as BD set-up:

Example 14 Track 40, 41, 42

A - As written:

B - Played as SD set-up:

C - Played as BD set-up:

There are more big band figures you will need to play, but in a swing feel they primarily fit into one or some combination of the eight 4/4 rhythms (exercises 1-8) or six 3/4 rhythms (exercises 9-14) presented in the previous section. You will have many opportunities to play multiple big band figures with the play-along charts. The goal of the big band set-ups is to clearly indicate to the rest of the band where the figure is to be played. Your set-up can either make this very clear or confuse the other musicians. Be sure you are comfortable playing each individual set-up in exercises 1-14 before playing these combination charts.

4/4 Combination Chart Track 43 & 61 (with embellishments)

3/4 Combination Chart Track 44 & 62 (with embellishments)

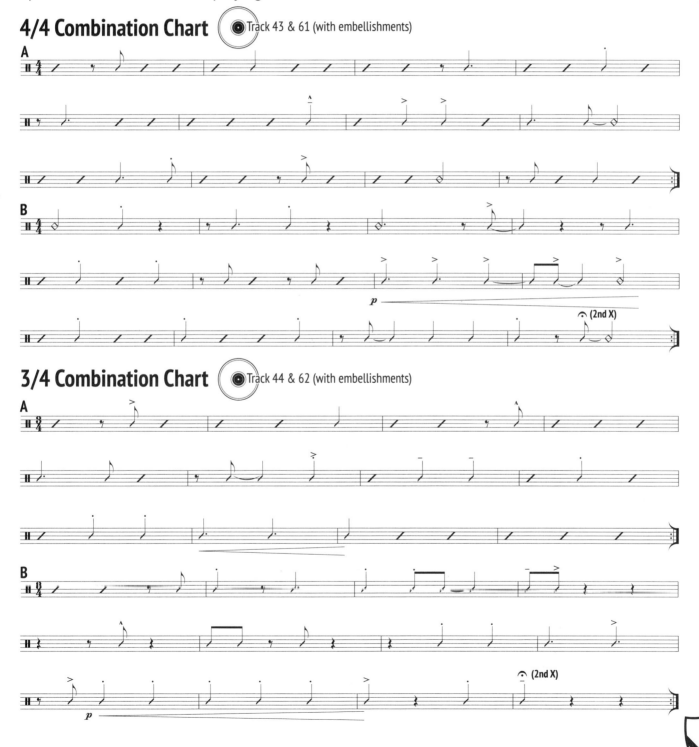

Part Six: Embellishing Your Set-Ups

Embellishing your set-ups means adding more than just a single note.
Following are sixteen examples of how to embellish a set-up for beat one. Be
sure to experiment with different combinations of drums and cymbal crashes. Try
playing more notes on the toms and bass drum to create a thicker sounding set-up.
Some set-ups work better at slower tempos while others work better at faster tempos.
Recorded music is your best avenue for learning more fills and creative orchestrations
with your set-ups. See the recommended listening section for a discography of
recordings to listen to and learn from.

1. Flams — Track 45 with exercise 1 @ 120 BPM

2. Drags — Track 46

3 Ruffs — Track 47

4. Shuffle — Track 48

5. Shuffle Flams — Track 49

6. Triplets — Track 50

7. The "Dump" Triplets — Track 51

Part Six

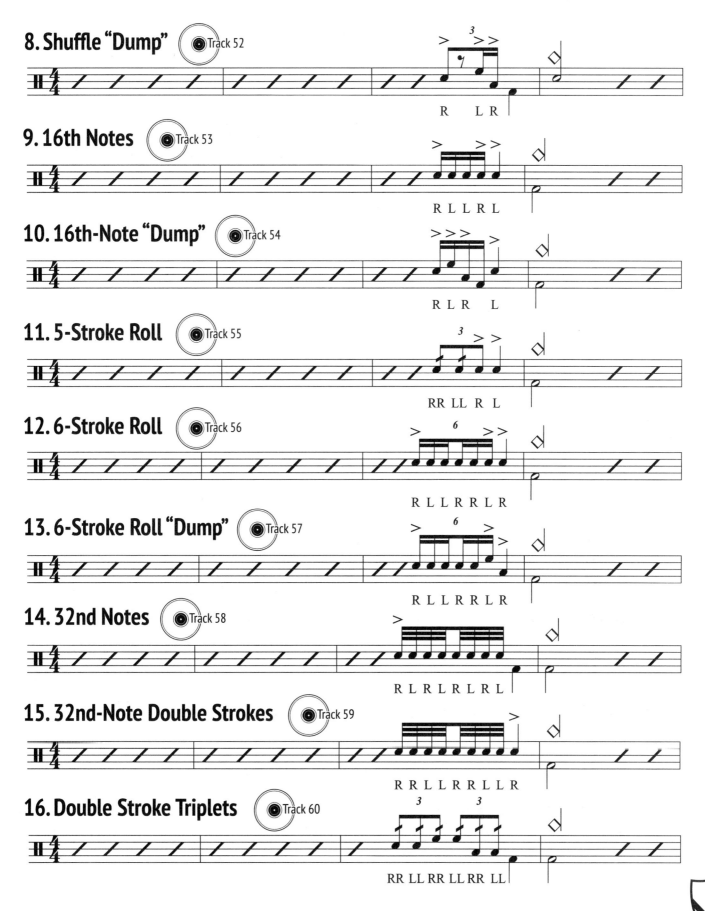

8. Shuffle "Dump" Track 52

9. 16th Notes Track 53

10. 16th-Note "Dump" Track 54

11. 5-Stroke Roll Track 55

12. 6-Stroke Roll Track 56

13. 6-Stroke Roll "Dump" Track 57

14. 32nd Notes Track 58

15. 32nd-Note Double Strokes Track 59

16. Double Stroke Triplets Track 60

Part Seven: Jazz Drumming Styles

Jazz music and jazz drumming styles have evolved for decades. From early styles through todays mix of so many genres of music, there are a number of jazz drumming styles in which to choose from. Your jazz drumming sound will be a combination of what you listen to and your drumset technique and coordination abilities. Your choice of cymbals, drums, grooves, fills, solos, dynamics and complexity should be in response to what you hear the musicians playing.

There are several important jazz drumming styles drummers need to learn. These jazz drumming styles will give you a place to start. Each style serves a unique purpose.

Groove Jazz - "Laying it down" or "Swingin' hard" — Track 63 (with exercise #1) @90 BPM & no horns

Riff Jazz - "AABA" or "Call and response" — Track 64 @ 120 BPM & no horns

Bebop Jazz - Syncopated interplay with snare, bass, and hi-hat — Track 65 @ 160 BPM & no horns

Shuffle Jazz - "chu-ga, Cha-ga, cha-gu, Cha-gu" — Track 66 @ 120 BPM & no horns

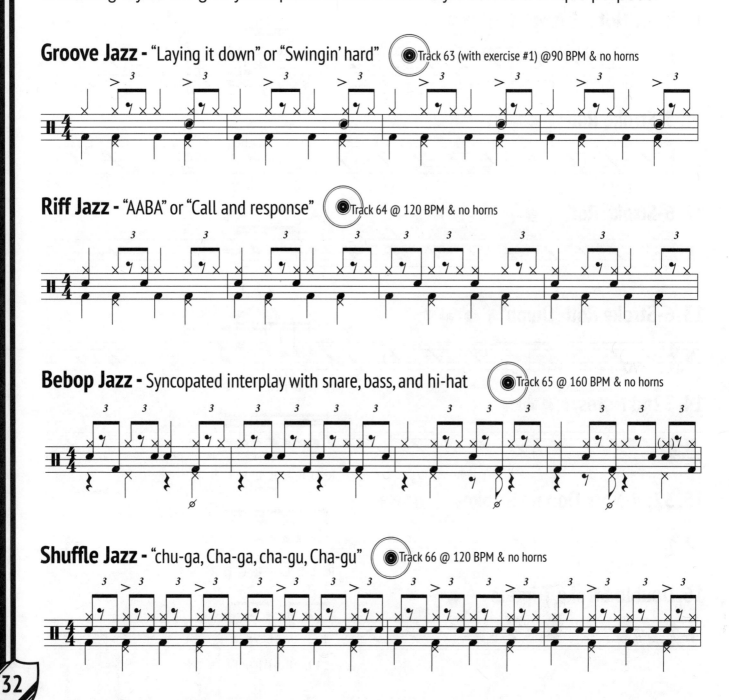

Part Seven

Double Shuffle - Slow tempos ⦿Track 67 @ 90 BPM & no horns

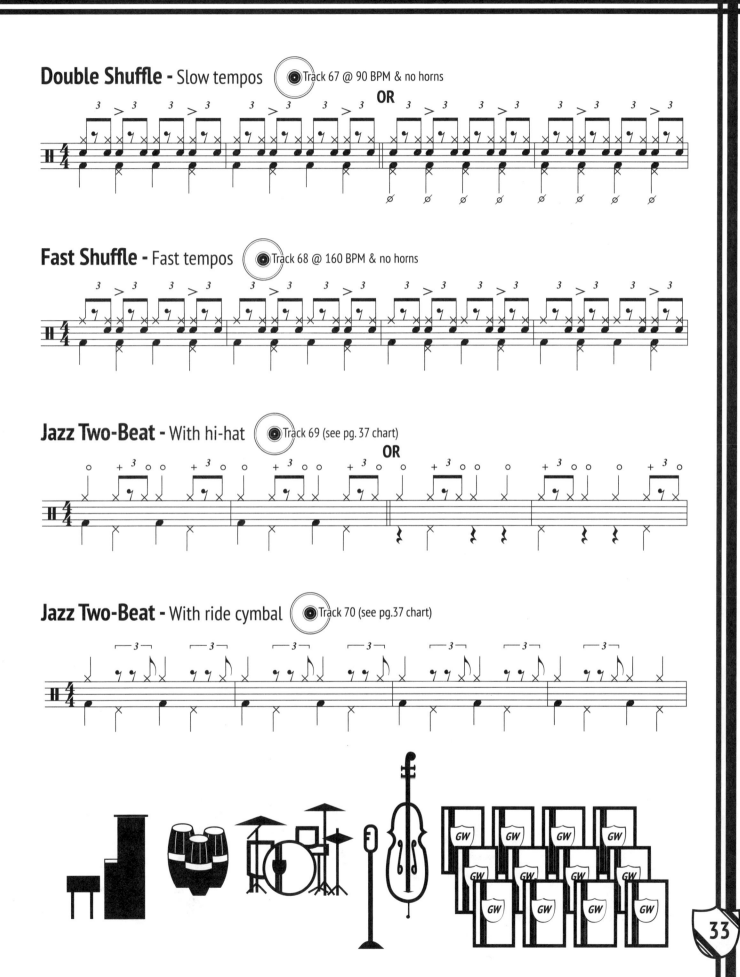

Fast Shuffle - Fast tempos ⦿Track 68 @ 160 BPM & no horns

Jazz Two-Beat - With hi-hat ⦿Track 69 (see pg. 37 chart)

Jazz Two-Beat - With ride cymbal ⦿Track 70 (see pg.37 chart)

Part Seven

2. 3/4 Swing

3/4 Jazz Waltz - In a walking 3 feel ⦿ Track 71 (see pg.37 chart)

3/4 Jazz in "1" - Creates a "floating" feel ⦿ Track 72 (see pg.37 chart)

3/4 Jazz in "2" - With a 2-against-3 polyrhythm ⦿ Track 73 (see pg.37 chart)

3. Brushes

Ballad ⦿ Track 74: 12/8 feel
75: 4/4 feel

All-Purpose ⦿ Track 76: @ 120 BPM & no horns
77: @ 160 BPM & no horns
78: 2-beat feel

(see pg. 37 chart)

(see pg. 37 chart)

Part Eight: Additional Drumming Styles

World beat, rhythm and blues (R&B), rock and funk styles are often incorporated into the big band repertoire. Today's big band drummer needs to have some knowledge and abilities in a variety of styles. Following are a few important grooves in several styles:

1. Traditional Afro Cuban 6/8 - With 3:2 Son Clave Track 79 (see pg. 38 chart)

2. Contemporary Afro Cuban 6/8 - With 3:2 Rhumba Clave Track 80

3. Bossa Nova - With 3:2 Bossa Clave Track 81

4. Samba Track 82

5. Salsa - With 2:3 Son Clave Track 83

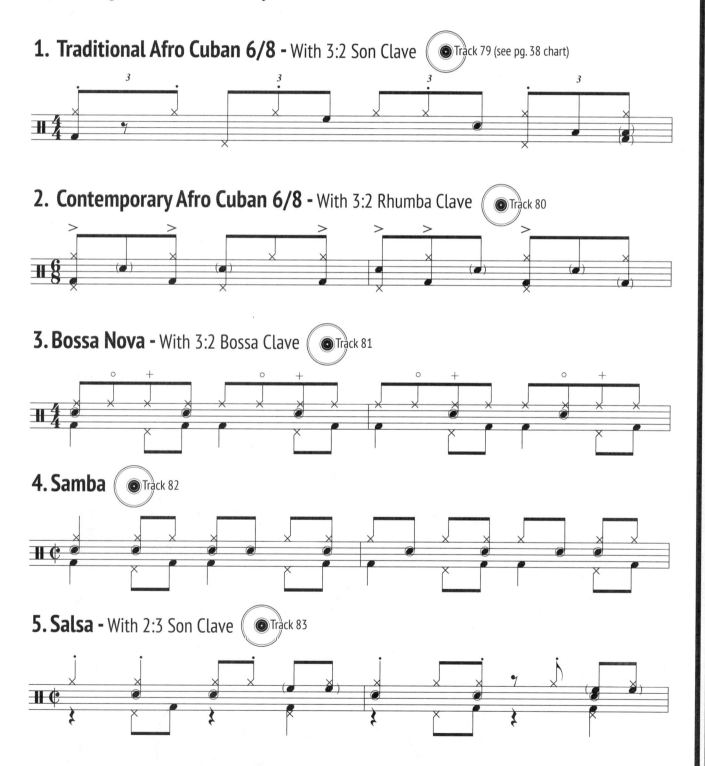

Part Eight

6. Rhumba  Track 84

7. 12/8 Rhythm & Blues (R&B) Track 85

8. Rock Shuffle Track 86 (see pg. 39 chart)

9. Funk Shuffle Track 87

10. Rock Track 88

11. R&B/Hip Hop Track 89

12. Funk Track 90

Part Eight

Band Chord Charts:

12-Bar Blues (works with 4/4 exercises, combination chart, jazz styles, shuffles, and the all-purpose brush stroke)

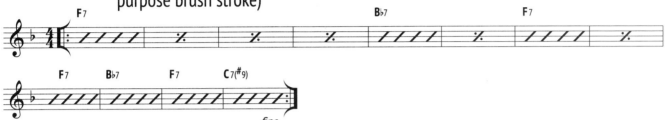

12-Bar Blues - Waltz (works with 3/4 exercises and 3/4 combination chart)

Two-Beat Swing (works with 2-beat hi-hat, ride, and brush strokes)

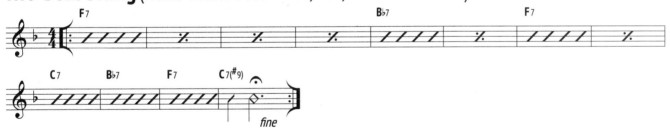

Waltz (works with 3/4 jazz in a "3" feel, "1" feel, and "2" feel)

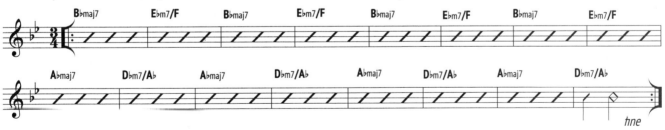

Ballad (works with 12/8 and 4/4 ballad brush strokes)

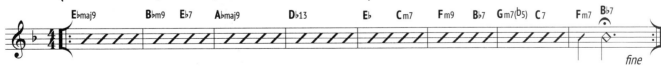

Part Eight

Afro Cuban 6/8 (works with traditional and contemporary 6/8 grooves)

Bossa Nova

Samba

Salsa

Rhumba

12/8 R&B

Part Eight

Rock Shuffle

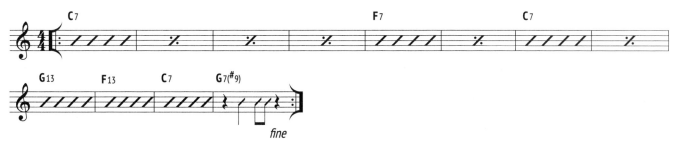

Funk Shuffle

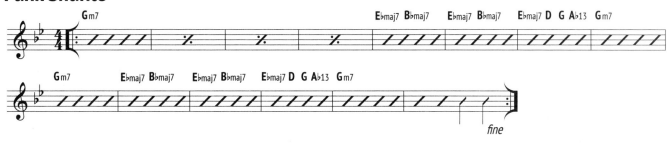

Rock

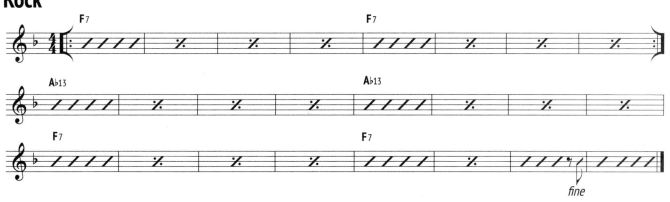

R&B/Hip Hop - Swing feel

Funk

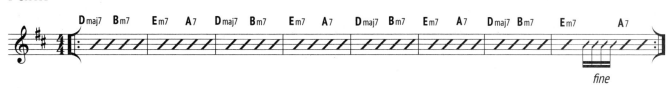

Part Nine: The Charts

There are five jazz charts that you can play along with. These charts include jazz shuffle, medium swing, slow swing, 3/4 swing and fast swing. Three charts are instrumental and two feature vocalists backed by the big band.

If you are a careful listener, you will notice that I pay ("play") close attention to:

Dynamics - I will play softer than the band if I can.

Articulations - I follow the short notes and create space in the sound.

Section Figures - I compliment on snare or bass drum and with the ride as well.

Ensemble Figures - I set up and "kick" with a crash.

Feel Changes - I change from a two-beat (hi-hat) to walking feel (ride), etc.

Cymbal Changes - Jazz is cymbal-driven music! Notice how I am changing ride cymbals and/or from hi-hat to ride cymbal at phrase points, as well as making cymbal changes to complement the form of the music and/or the soloist.

Horn Colors - I am changing cymbals to match the changing soloists and the sound of their instrument:

High Brass = Higher ride
Low Brass = Lower ride
Saxophone = China or a darker sounding ride.
(Note: The China works especially well behind a saxophone soli.)

My playing is a reaction to what I hear going on around me combined with the information on the chart. John Moawad would say, "The best skill any musician can have is a great pair of ears!!" Many of the great musicians of the past did not know how to read music. They sounded so good because they listened and played music more than they read about it.

There is a saying, "A picture paints a thousand words." I say, "A recording paints a thousand notes." Learn to hear with your eyes. Here's how...

First: Listen to the CD track while following along with the chart. This will help you understand how I arrived at the drum parts I played. Make any notes you need to on the chart, circle or highlight the dynamic markings, circle the long notes that you want to crash, write the cymbal changes at the phrase points, circle the DS or DC, etc.

Second: Play along with the track that I am playing to and see if you can imitate what I am playing.

Third: Play along with the version of the chart that doesn't have my drum part. This way you can use my ideas and/or create your own.

Adjust the tempos. You may consider slowing some of these tracks down with a tempo adjustment app such as: The Amazing Slow Downer or Tempo Slow Mo, etc. Having the ability to adjust the tempo is a great way to bring the song to a more comfortable tempo before trying it at full tempo or increasing the tempo for a different vibe or to challenge yourself more.

The charts are: ⊙ Track 91 - 101

"Bella's Boogie" - jazz shuffle (91, 92)
"Just You, Just Me" - medium swing with brushes and sticks (93, 94)
"Ramblin'" - slow swing (95, 96)
"Wheel" - 3/4 swing (97. 98)
"Undecided" - fast swing (99, 100)
"Strike Up the Band" - *bonus track from 1984 (101)

Part Nine

Track 91, 92

Bella's Boogie

Jim Cutler

Shuffle ♩=116

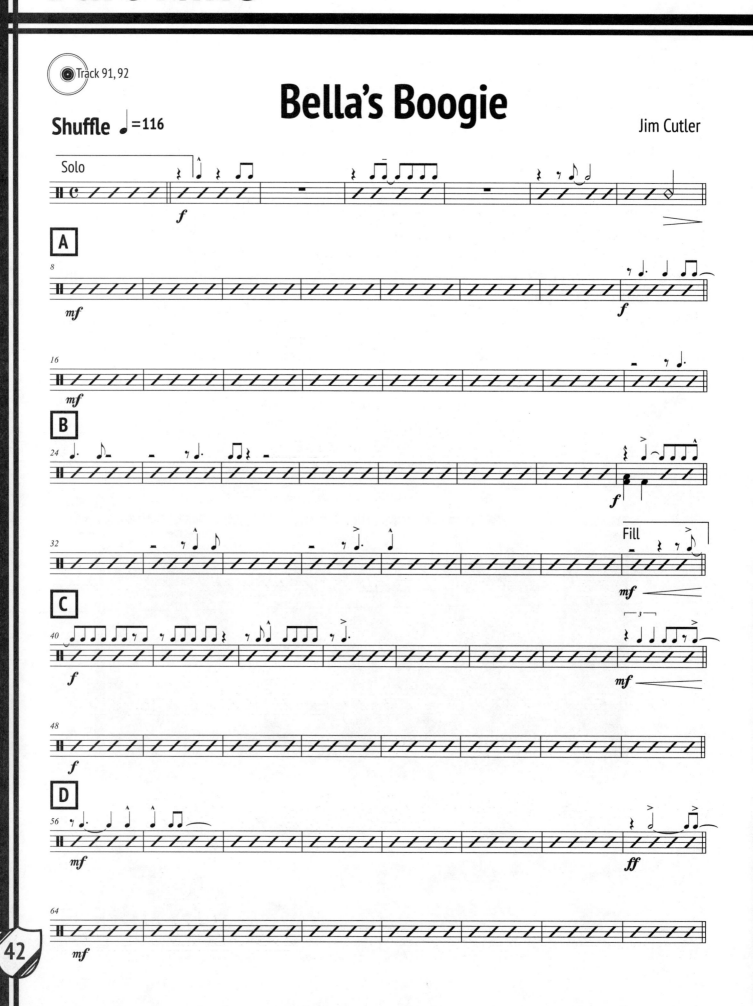

Part Nine

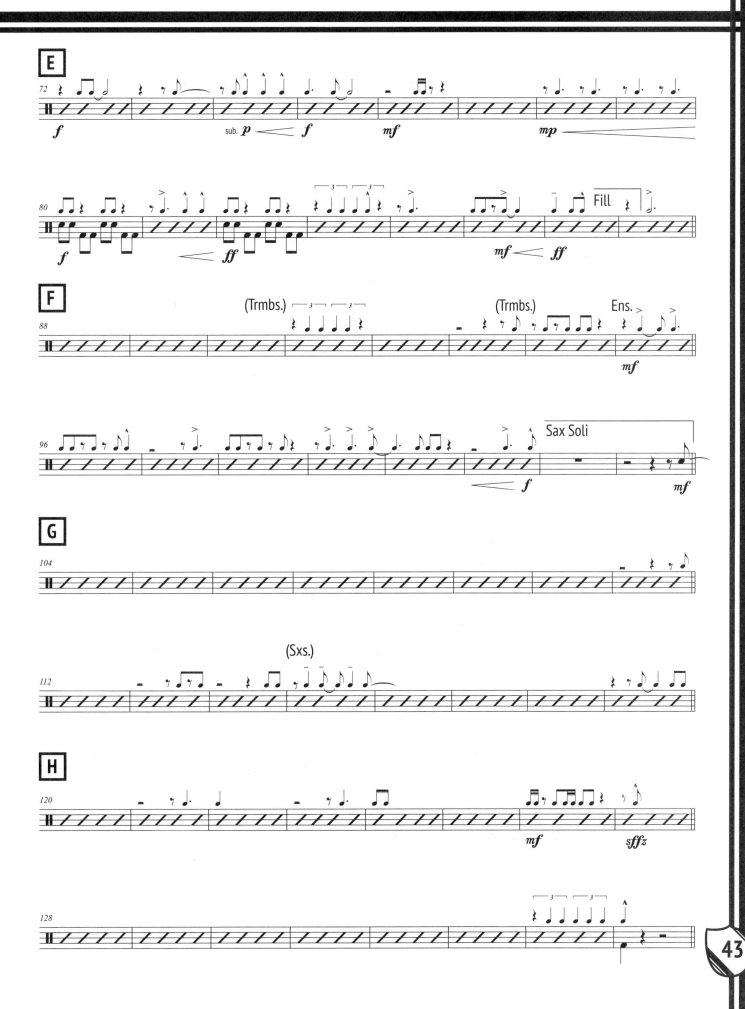

Part Nine

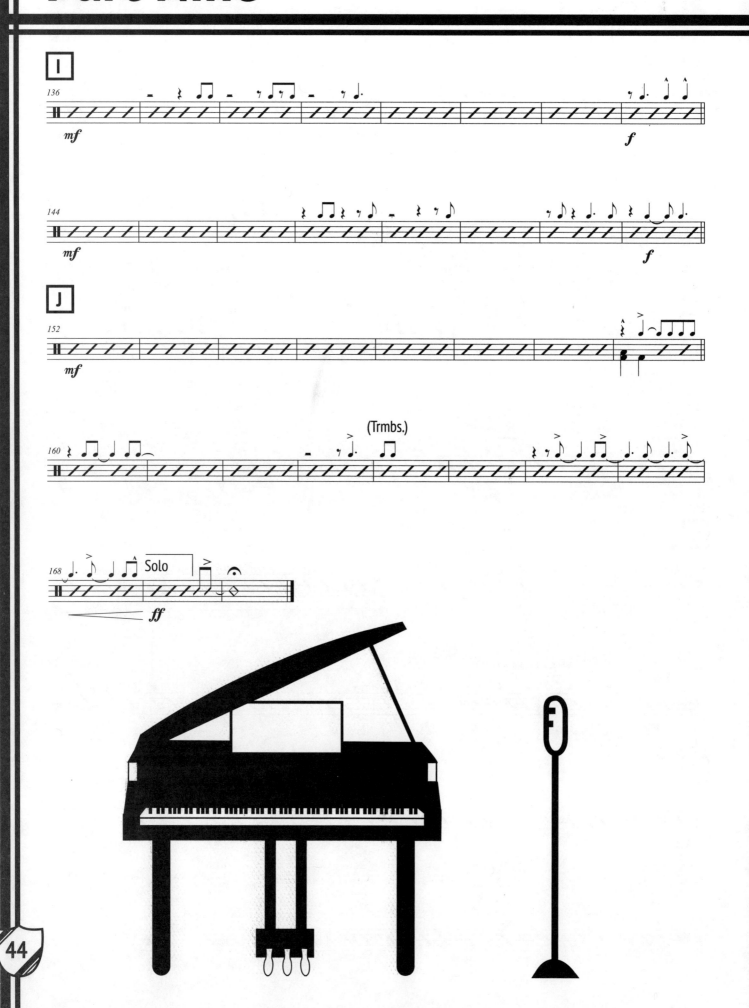

Part Nine

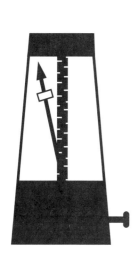

"We're all on the same bus, and you're the bus driver"

\- John Moawad

Part Nine

Just You, Just Me

for Warren Balfour
and the Royal Garden Swing Orchestra

arr. George Stone

Medium Swing ♩= 116

Part Nine

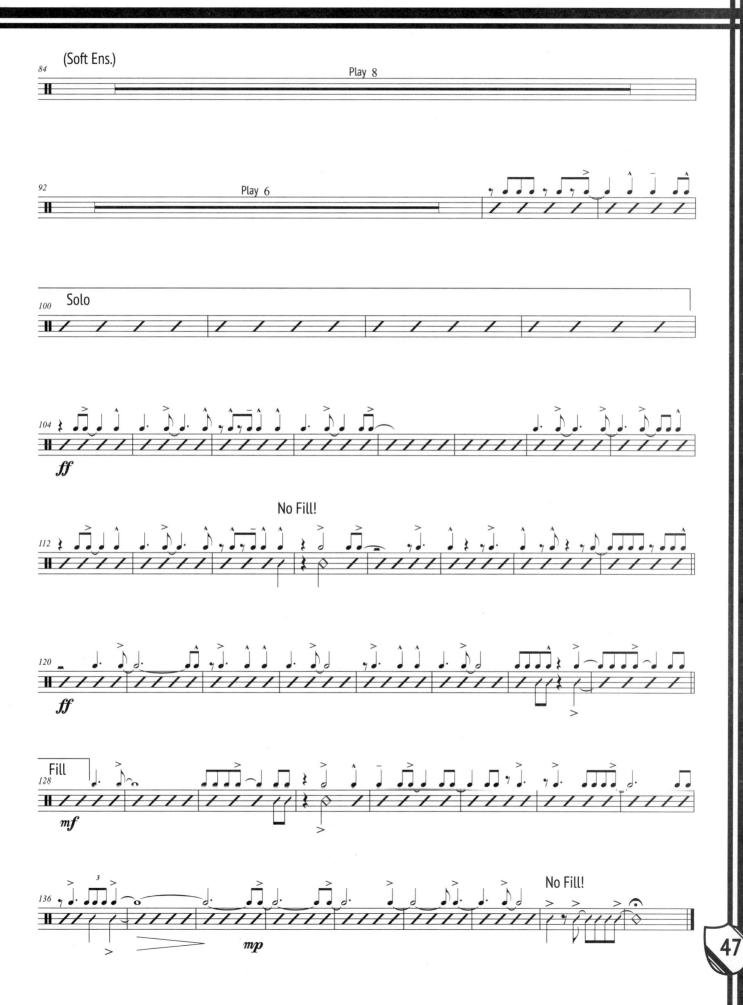

Part Nine

Track 95, 96

Ramblin'

Slow Swing

arr. Bob Hammer

"Some things can't be taught, they have to be caught"

- John Moawad

Part Nine

Track 97, 98

Wheel

3/4 Swing

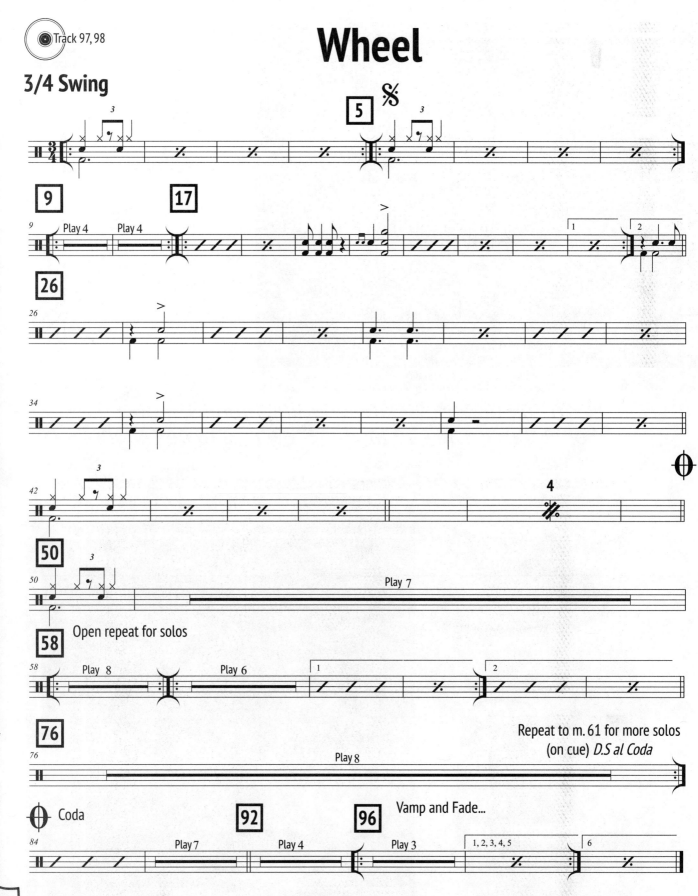

"Practicing means working on things you can't do"

- John Moawad

Part Nine

Undecided

Fast Swing

Charlie Shavers
arr. Bob Hammer

Part Nine

" There is no such thing as almost "

- John Moawad

Burton J. Williams, Dizzy Gillespie, and Garey Williams, 1983

Discography

Following are some selected CD listening recommendations for big band styles:

Count Basie - *Live at the Sands* (Sonny Payne)
Reprise 9 45946-2

Louie Bellson - *Big Band Dynamite* (Louie Bellson)
Concord Jazz CCD-4105

Louie Bellson - *The Louie Bellson Explosion* (Louie Bellson)
Pablo OJCCD-728-2 (2310-735)

The Frank Capp Juggernaut - *In a Hefti Bag* (Frank Capp)
Concord Jazz CCD-4655

The Frank Capp Juggernaut - *Play It Again Sam* (Frank Capp)
Concord Jazz CCD-4747-2

Clarke-Boland Big Band - *Handle with Care* (Kenny Clarke)
KOCH Jazz KOC CD-8534

Clayton-Hamilton Jazz Orchestra - *Shout Me Out* (Jeff Hamilton)
Fable Records 54395-2

Clayton-Hamilton Jazz Orchestra - *Live At MCG* (Jeff Hamilton)
MCGJ1017

Maynard Ferguson - *The Birdland Dream Band Vol. 2* (Don Lamond)
BMG (Spain) RCA 74321580572

Terry Gibbs Dream Band - *Flying Home Vol. 3* (Mel Lewis)
Contemporary CCD-7654-2

Terry Gibbs Dream Band - *The Sundown Sessions Vol. 2* (Mel Lewis)
Contemporary CCD-7652-2

Woody Herman - *Verve Jazz Masters 54* (Jake Hanna)
Verve 314 529 903-2

Stan Kenton Orchestra - *Live At Brigham Young University* (John Von Ohlen)
Creative World STD 1039

The Buddy Rich Big Band - *Swingin' New Band* (Buddy Rich)
Pacific Jazz CDP 7243 8 35232 2 1

The Buddy Rich Big Band - *Big Swing Face* (Buddy Rich)
Pacific Jazz CDP 7243 8 37989 2 6

CD Track List

The latest great books from Wizdom Media:

NEW! Arrival Drum Play-Along (Book/MP3 Disc) by Joe Bergamini with Dom Famularo: With exciting rock, funk, and progressive tracks taken from Joe's 1996 debut album. Featuring Zak Rizvi and Frank LaPlaca from 4Front, all 10 tracks contain complete charts with suggested grooves and fills, as well as audio versions with drums, minus drums with click, and minus click without drums.

NEW! The Pulse of Jazz (Book/MP3 Disc) by Nic Marcy: A complete, cutting-edge approach to jazz timekeeping from basic to very advanced. Includes extensive audio and video examples, plus play-along tracks!

Odd Feelings **(Book/MP3 Disc) by Massimo Russo and Dom Famularo:** A complete, easy-to-understand approach to odd time signatures. With play-along tracks, MP3 examples and QuickTime videos.

The Hi-Hat Foot **(Book/MP3 Disc) by Garey Williams:** Gain faciliy with your weakest limb by practicing this complete set of grooves for rock and funk with practical hi-hat foot patterns.

Groove Facility **(Book/MP3 Disc) by Rob Hirons and Dom Famularo:** Build a funky vocabulary of grooves using a library of one-beat components. Clearly explains Moeller motions and strokes. Included multi-media disc contains MP3 examples and QuickTime videos.

Open-Handed Playing Vol. 2: A Step Beyond **(Book/CD) by Claus Hessler with Dom Famularo:** Follow-up to the popular first volume, with clear explanations of the linear and rudimental approaches to OHP. Includes 8 new play-along tracks.

ALSO AVAILABLE:
- *Drumset Duets* by Dom Famularo with Stephane Chamberland (Book/MP3 Disc)
- *Elements* (Book/MP3 Disc) by John Favicchia
- *Pedal Control* (Book/MP3 & Video Disc) by Dom Famularo and Joe Bergamini
- *Open-Handed Playing* (Book/CD) by Claus Hessler with Dom Famularo
- *The Weaker Side* (Book) by Dom Famularo and Stephane Chamberland
- *Eighth-Note Rock and Beyond* (Book/MP3 Disc) by Glenn Ceglia with Dom Famularo

WIZDOM MEDIA

www.wizdom-media.com
Wizdom Media LLC
PO Box 45, Whippany NJ 07981
Exclusively distributed by Alfred Music Publishing Co.
Available at fine music stores and online retailers